# On Continence

# On Continence

## St. Augustine

# On Continence

© Lighthouse Publishing 2018

Written by: St. Augustine (Nov.13 354 – Aug.28 430)

Translated by: Rev. C. L. Cornish. M.A.

Updated into Modern U.S English by A.M. Overett (b. 1960)

All rights reserved. Without limiting the rights under copyright reserved above, no part of this publication may be reproduced, stored in a retrieval system, or transmitted, in any form or by any means (electronic, mechanical, photocopying, recording or otherwise), without the prior written permission of the copyright owner of this book.

Published by
Lighthouse Christian Publishing
SAN 257-4330
5531 Dufferin Drive
Savage, Minnesota, 55378
United States of America

www.lighthousechristianpublishing.com

1. It is difficult to treat of the virtue of the soul, which is called Continence, in a manner fully suitable and worthy; but He, whose great gift this virtue is, will help our littleness under the burden of so great a weight. For He, who bestows it upon His faithful ones when they are continent, Himself gives discourse of it to His ministers when they speak. Lastly, of so great a matter purposing to speak what Himself shall grant, in the first place we say and prove that Continence is the gift of God. We have it written in the Book of Wisdom, that no one can be continent, unless God grant it. But the Lord, concerning that greater and more glorious Continence itself, whereby there is continence from the marriage bond, says, "Not all can receive this saying, but they to whom it is given." And since marriage chastity also itself cannot be guarded, unless there be Continence from unlawful intercourse, the Apostle declared both to be the gift of God, when He spoke of both lives, that is, both that of marriage and that without marriage, saying, "I would that all men were so as myself; but each hath his own gift from God; one in this manner, another in that manner."

2. And lest it should seem that necessary Continence was to be hoped for from the Lord only in respect of the lust of the lower parts of the flesh, it is also sung in the Psalm; "Set, O Lord, a watch to my mouth, and a door of Continence around my lips." But in this witness of the divine speech, if we understand "mouth" as we ought to understand it, we perceive how great a gift of God Continence there set is. Forsooth it is little to contain the mouth of the body, lest anything burst forth thence, which is not for the better, through the sound of the voice. For there is, within, the mouth of the heart, where he, who

spoke these words, and wrote them for us to speak, desired of the Lord that the watch and door of Continence should be set for him. For many things we say not with the mouth of the body, and cry aloud with the heart: but there goes forth from the mouth of the body no word of anything, whereof there is silence in the heart. Therefore what flows not forth thence, sounds not abroad: but what flows forth thence, if it be evil, although it move not the tongue, defiles the soul. Therefore Continence must be set there, where the conscience even of them who are silent speaks. For it is brought to pass by means of the door of Continence, that there go not forth thence that, which, even when the lips of the flesh are closed, pollutes the life of him that hath the thought.

3. Lastly, to show more plainly the inner mouth, which by these words he meant, after having said, "Set a watch, O Lord, to my mouth, and a door of Continence around my lips," he added straightway, "Cause not my heart to fall aside into evil words." The falling aside of the heart, what is it but the consent? For he hath not yet spoken, whosoever in his heart hath with no falling aside of the heart consented unto suggestions that meet him of each several thing that is seen. But, if he hath consented, he hath already spoken in his heart, although he hath not uttered sound by the mouth; although he hath not done with hand or any part whatever of the body, yet hath he done what in his thought he hath already determined that he is to do: guilty by the divine laws, although hidden to human senses; the word having been spoken in the heart, no deed having been committed through the body. But in no case would he have moved the limb without, in a deed, the beginning of which deed had not gone before within

in word. For it is no lie that is written, that "the beginning of every work is a word." Forsooth men do many things with mouth closed, tongue quiet, voice bridled; but yet they do nothing by work of the body, which they have not before spoken in the heart. And through this since there are many sins in inward sayings which are not in outward deeds, whereas there are none in outward deeds, which do not go before in inward sayings, there will be purity of innocence from both, if the door of Continence be set around the inward lips.

4. For which cause our Lord Himself also with His own mouth says, "Cleanse what are within, and what are without will be clean." And, also, in another place, when He was refuting the foolish speeches of the Jews, in that they spoke evil against His disciples, eating with unwashed hands; "Not what enters into the mouth," said He, "defiles the man: but what cometh forth out of the mouth, that defiles the man." Which sentence, if the whole of it be taken of the mouth of the body, is absurd. For neither doth vomit defile him, whom food defiles not. Forsooth food enters into the mouth, vomit proceeds forth out of the mouth. But without doubt the former words relate to the mouth of the flesh, where He says, "Not what enters into the mouth defiles the man," but the latter words to the mouth of the heart, where He saith, "But what proceeds forth out of the mouth, this defiles the man." Lastly, when the Apostle Peter sought of Him an explanation of this as of a parable, He answered, "Are ye also yet without understanding? understand ye not, that whatsoever enters into the mouth, goes into the belly, and is cast out into the draught?" Here surely we perceive the mouth of the flesh, into which the food enters. But in

what He next adds, in order that we might recognize the mouth of the heart, the slowness of our heart would not follow, did not the Truth deign to walk even with the slow. For He saith, "But what things go forth from the mouth, go out of the heart;" as though He should say, When you hear it said "from the mouth," understand "from the heart." I say both, but I set forth one by the other. The inner man hath an inner mouth, and this the inner ear discerns: what things go forth from this mouth, go out of the heart, and they defile the man. Then having left the term mouth, which may be understood also of the body, He shows more openly what He is saying. "For from the heart go out," saith He, "evil thoughts, murders, adulteries, fornications, thefts, false witness, blasphemies; these are what defile the man." There is surely no one of those evils, which can be committed also by the members of the body, but that the evil thoughts go before and defile the man, although something hinder the sinful and wicked deeds of the body from following. For if, because power is not given, the hand is free from the murder of a man, is the heart of the murderer forsooth therefore clean from sin? Or if she be chaste, whom one unchaste wishes to commit adultery with, hath he on that account failed to commit adultery with her in his heart? Or if the harlot be not found in the brothel, doth he, who seeks her, on that account fail to commit fornication in his heart? Or if time and place be wanting to one who wishes to hurt his neighbor by a lie, hath he on that account failed already to speak false witness with his inner mouth? Or if anyone fearing men, dare not utter aloud blasphemy with tongue of flesh, is he on this account guiltless of this crime, who saith in his heart, "There is no God." Thus all the other evil deeds of men, which no motion of the body performs, of which no sense of the body is conscious, have their own secret criminals, who are also polluted by consent alone in thought, that is, by evil words of the inner mouth. Into which he (the Psalmist) fearing lest his heart should fall aside, asks of the Lord that the door of Continence be set around the lips of this mouth, to contain the heart, that it fall not aside into evil words: but contain it, by not suffering thought to proceed to consent: for thus, according to the precept of the Apostle, sin reigns not in our mortal body, nor do we yield our members as weapons of unrighteousness unto sin. From fulfilling which precept they are surely far removed, who on this account turn not their members to sin, because no power is allowed them; and if this be present, straightway by the motions of their members, as of weapons, they show, who reigns in them within. Wherefore so far as is in themselves, they yield their members weapons of unrighteousness unto sin; because this is what they wish, which for this reason they yield not, because they are not able.

5. And on this account that, which, the parts that beget being bridled by modesty, is most chiefly and properly to be called Continence, is violated by no transgression, if the higher Continence, concerning which we have been some time speaking, be preserved in the heart. For this reason the Lord, after He had said, "For from the heart go forth evil thoughts," then went on to add what it is that belongs to evil thoughts, "murders, adulteries," and the rest. He spoke not of all; but, having named certain by way of instance, He taught that we are to understand others also. Of which there is no one that can take place, unless an evil thought have gone before,

whereby that is prepared within which is done without, and going forth out of the mouth of the heart already defiles the man, although, through no power being granted, it be not done without by means of the members of the body. When therefore a door of Continence hath been set in the mouth of the heart, whence go out all that defile the man, if nothing such be permitted to go out thence, there followed a purity, wherein now the conscience may rejoice; although there be not as yet that perfection, wherein Continence shall not strive with vice. But now, so long as "the flesh lusted against the spirit, and the spirit against the flesh," it is enough for us not to consent unto the evils which we feel in us. But, when that consent takes place, then there goes out of the mouth of the heart what defiles the man. But when through Continence consent is withheld, the evil of the lust of the flesh, against which the lust of the spirit fights, is not suffered to harm.

6. But it is one thing to fight well, which now is, when the strife of death is resisted; another thing not to have an adversary, which will then be, when death, "the last enemy," shall be destroyed. For Continence also itself, when it curbs and restrains lusts, at once both seeks the good unto the immortality of which we aim, and rejects the evil with which in this mortality we contend. Of the one it is forsooth the lover and beholder, but of the other both the enemy and witness: both seeking what becomes, and fleeing what misbecomes. Assuredly Continence would not labor in curbing lusts, if we had no wishes contrary to what is becoming, if there were no opposition on the part of evil lust unto our good will. The Apostle cries aloud, "I know," saith he, "that there

dwelleth not in me, that is in my flesh, good. For to will lies near to me, but to accomplish good I find not." For now good can be done, so far as that there be no assent given unto evil lust: but good will be accomplished, when the evil lust itself shall come to an end. And also the same teacher of the Gentiles cries aloud, "I take pleasure together with the law of God after the inner man: but I see another law in my members, warring against the law of my mind."

7. This conflict none experience in themselves, save such as war on the side of the virtues, and war down the vices: nor doth anything storm the evil of lust, save the good of Continence. But there are, who, being utterly ignorant of the law of God, account not evil lusts among their enemies, and through wretched blindness being slaves to them, over and above think themselves also blessed, by satisfying them rather than taming them. But whoso through the Law have come to know them, ("For through the Law is the knowledge of sin," and, "Lust," saith he, "I knew not, unless the Law should say, Thou shalt not lust after," and yet are overcome by their assault, because they live under the Law, whereby what is good is commanded, but not also given: they live not under Grace, which gives through the Holy Spirit what is commanded through the Law: unto these the Law therefore entered, that in them the offense might abound. The prohibition increased the lust, and made it unconquered: that there might be transgression also, which without the Law was not, although there was sin, "For where there is not Law, neither is there transgression." Thus the Law, Grace not helping, forbidding sin, became over and above the strength of sin;

whence the Apostle saith, "The Law is the strength of sin." Nor is it to be wondered at, that man's weakness even from the good Law added strength to evil, whilst it trusts to fulfill the Law itself of its own strength. Forsooth being ignorant of the righteousness of God, which He gives unto the weak, and wishing to establish his own, of which the weak is void, he was not made subject to the righteousness of God, reprobate and proud. But if the Law, as a schoolmaster, lead unto Grace one made an offender, as though for this purpose more grievously wounded, that he may desire a Physician; against the baneful sweetness, whereby lust prevailed, the Lord gives a sweetness that worketh good, that by it Continence may the more delight, and "our land giveth her fruit," whereby the soldier is fed, who by the help of the Lord wars down sin.

8. Such soldiers the Apostolic trumpet enkindles for battle with that sound, "Therefore let not," saith he, "sin reign in your mortal body to obey its lusts; nor yield your members weapons of unrighteousness unto sin; but yield yourselves unto God, as living in place of dead, and your members weapons of righteousness unto God. For sin shall not rule over you. For ye are not under the law, but under Grace." And in another place, "Therefore," saith he, "brethren, we are debtors, not to the flesh, to live after the flesh. For if ye shall live after the flesh, ye shall die; but if by the Spirit ye shall mortify the deeds of the flesh, ye shall live. For as many as are led by the Spirit of God, these are sons of God." This therefore is the business in hand, so long as this our mortal life under Grace lasts, that sin, that is the lust of sin, (for this he in this place calls by the name of sin,) reign not in this our

mortal body. But it is then shown to reign, if obedience be yielded to its desires. There is therefore in us lust of sin, which must not be suffered to reign; there are its desires, which we must not obey, lest obeying it reign over us. Wherefore let not lust usurp our members, but let Continence claim them for herself; that they be weapons of righteousness unto God, that they be not weapons of unrighteousness unto sin; for thus sin shall not rule over us. For we are not under the Law, which indeed commanded what is good yet giveth it not: but we are under Grace, which, making us to love that which the Law commands, is able to rule over the free.

9. And also, when he exhorts us, that we live not after the flesh, lest we die, but that by the Spirit we mortify the deeds of the flesh, that we may live; surely the trumpet which sounds, shows the war in which we are engaged, and enkindles us to contend keenly, and to do our enemies to death, that we be not done to death by them. But who those enemies are, it hath set forth plainly enough. For those are they, whom it willed should be done to death by us, that is to say, the works of the flesh. For so it saith, "But if by the Spirit ye shall mortify the deeds of the flesh, ye shall live." And in order that we may know what these are, let us hear the same in like manner writing unto the Galatians, and saying, "But the works of the flesh are manifest, which are, fornications, uncleannesses, luxuries, idolatry, witchcrafts, hatreds, contentions, emulations, wraths, strifes, heresies, envyings, drunkennesses, revellings, and such like; of which I foretell to you, as I have foretold, that they who do such things shall not possess the kingdom of God." For the very war there also was he showing, that he should

speak of these, and unto the death-doing of these enemies was he calling up the soldiers of Christ by the same heavenly and spiritual trumpet. For he had said above, "But I say, walk in the Spirit, and perform ye not the lusts of the flesh. For the flesh lusted against the Spirit, and the Spirit against the flesh. For these are opposed one to the other, that ye do not what ye would. But if ye are led by the Spirit, ye are not under the Law." Therefore being set under Grace, he would have them have that conflict against the works of the flesh. And in order to point out these works of the flesh, he added what I have mentioned above. "But the works of the flesh are manifest, which are, fornications," and the rest, whether what he mentioned, or whether what he admonished were to be understood, chiefly as he added, "and such like." Lastly, in this battle, against what is in a manner the carnal army leading forth as it were another spiritual line, "But the fruit of the Spirit is," saith he, "charity, joy, peace, long-suffering, kindness, goodness, faith, gentleness, continence; against such there is no law." He saith not "against these," lest they should be thought to be alone: although even were he to say this, we ought to understand all, whatever goods of the same kind we could think of: but he saith, "against such," that is to say, both these and whatsoever are such like. However, in that among the goods of which he made mention, he set Continence in the last place, (concerning which we have now undertaken to treat, and on account of which we have already said much,) he willed that it should in an especial manner cleave to our minds. Forsooth this same is of great avail in this case, wherein the Spirit lusted against the flesh; forasmuch as in a certain way it crucifies the lusts of the flesh. Whence, after the Apostle had thus spoken, he added straightway, "But they who are Jesus Christ's have crucified their own flesh, with the passions and lusts." This is the acting of Continence: thus the works of the flesh are done to death. But they do to death those, whom falling away from Continence lust draws into consent to do such works.

10. But in order that we fall not away from Continence, we ought to watch specially against those snares of the suggestions of the devil, that we presume not of our own strength. For, "Cursed is every one that sets his hope in man." And who is he, but man? We cannot therefore truly say that he set not his hope in man, who sets it in himself. For this also, to "live after man," what is it but to "live after the flesh?" Whoso therefore is tempted by such a suggestion, let him hear, and, if he have any Christian feeling, let him tremble. Let him hear, I say, "If ye shall live after the flesh, ye shall die."

11. But someone will say to me that it is one thing to live after man, another thing to live after the flesh; because man forsooth is a rational creature, and there is in him a rational soul, whereby he differs from the beast: but the flesh is the lowest and earthly part of man, and thus to live after it is faulty: and for this reason, he who lives after man, assuredly lives not after the flesh, but rather after that part of man, whereby he is man, that is, after the spirit of the mind whereby he excels the beasts. But this discussion is perhaps of some force in the schools of philosophers: but we, in order to understand the Apostle of Christ, ought to observe in what manner the Christian books are used to speak; at any rate it is the belief of all of us, to whom to live is Christ, that Man was taken unto

Himself by the Word of God, not surely without a rational soul, as certain heretics will have it; and yet we read, "The Word was made flesh." What is to be here understood by "flesh," but Man? "And all flesh shall see the salvation of God." What can be understood, but all men? "Unto Thee shall all flesh come." What is it, but all men? "Thou hast given unto Him power over all flesh." What is it, but all men? "Of the works of the Law shall no flesh be justified." What is it, but no man shall be justified? And this the same Apostle in another place confessing more plainly saith, "Man shall not be justified of the works of the Law." The Corinthians also he rebukes, saying, "Are ye not carnal, and walk after man?" After he had called them carnal, he saith not, ye walk after the flesh, but after man, forasmuch as by this also what would he have understood, but after the flesh? For surely if to walk, that is, to live, after the flesh deserved blame, but after man deserved praise, he would not say by way of rebuke, "ye walk after man." Let man recognize the reproach; let him change his purpose, let him shun destruction. Hear thou man: walk not thou after man, but after Him Who made man. Fall not thou away from Him Who made thee, even unto thyself. For a man said, who yet lived not after man, "Not that we are sufficient to think anything from ourselves, as though of ourselves: but our sufficiency is of God." Consider if he lived after man, who spoke these things with truth. Therefore the Apostle, admonishing man not to live after man, restores man to God. But whoso lives not after man, but after God, assuredly lives not even after himself, because himself also is a man. But he is therefore said also to live after the flesh, when he so lives; because also when the flesh alone hath been named, man is understood, as we have already shown: just as when the soul alone hath been named, man is understood: whence it is said, "Let every soul be subject unto the higher powers," that is, every man; and, "Seventy-five souls went down into Egypt with Jacob," that is, seventy-five men. Therefore, live thou not after thyself, O man: thou has thence perished, but thou was sought. Live not then, I say, after thyself, O man; thou has thence perished, but thou was found. Accuse not thou the nature of the flesh, when you hear it said, "If ye shall live after the flesh, ye shall die." For thus could it be said, and most truly could it, If ye shall live after yourselves ye shall die. For the devil hath not flesh, and yet, because he would live after himself, "he abode not in the truth." What wonder therefore, if, living after himself, "when he spoke a lie, he spoke of his own," which the Truth spoke truly of him.

12. When, therefore, you hear it said, "Sin shall not reign over you;" have not thou confidence of thyself, that sin reign not over thee, but of Him, unto Whom a certain Saint saith in prayer, "Direct my paths after Thy Word, and let no iniquity have dominion over me." For lest haply, after that we had heard, "sin shall not reign over you," we should lift up ourselves, and lay this to our own strength, straightway the Apostle saw this, and added, "For ye are not under the Law, but under Grace." Therefore, Grace caused that sin reign not over you. Do not thou, therefore, have confidence of thyself, lest it thence reign much more over thee. And, when we hear it said, "If by the Spirit ye shall mortify the deeds of the flesh, ye shall live," let us not lay this so great good unto our own spirit, as though of itself it can do this. For, in order that we should not entertain that carnal sense, the

spirit being dead rather than that which putts others to death, straightway he added, "For as many as are led by the Spirit of God, these are sons of God." Therefore, that by our spirit we may mortify the works of the flesh, we are led by the Spirit of God, Who gives Continence, whereby to curb, tame, overcome lust.

13. In this so great conflict, wherein man under Grace lives, and when, being aided, he fights well, rejoices in the Lord with trembling, there yet are not wanting even to valiant warriors, and mortifiers however unconquered of the works of the flesh, some wounds of sins, for the healing of which they may say daily, "Forgive us our debts:" against the same vices, and against the devil the prince and king of vices, striving with much greater watchfulness and keenness by the very prayer, that his deadly suggestions avail not aught, whereby he further urges the sinner to excuse rather than accuse his own sins; and thus those wounds not only be not healed, but also, although they were not deadly, yet may be pressed home to grievous and fatal harm. And here therefore there is need of a more cautious Continence, whereby to restrain the proud appetite of man; whereby he is self-pleased, and unwilling to be found worthy of blame, and disdains, when he sins, to be convicted that he himself has sinned; not with healthful humility taking upon him to accuse himself, but rather with fatal arrogance seeking to find an excuse. In order to restrain this pride, he, whose words I have already set down above, and, as I could, commended, sought Continence from the Lord. For, after that he had said, "Set, O Lord, a watch to my mouth, and a door of Continence around my lips. Make not my heart to fall

aside unto evil words;" explaining more clearly whereof he spoke this, he saith, "to make excuses in sins." For what more evil than these words, whereby the evil man denies that he is evil, although convicted of an evil work, which he cannot deny. And since he cannot hide the deed, or say that it is well done, and still sees that it is clear that it was done by him, he seeks to refer to another what he hath done, as though he could remove thence what he hath deserved. Being unwilling that himself be guilty, he rather adds to his guilt, and by excusing, not accusing, his own sins, he knows not that he is putting from him, not punishment, but pardon. For before human judges, forasmuch as they may be deceived, it seems to profit somewhat for the time, to cleanse as it were what hath been done amiss by any deceit whatever; but before God, Who cannot be deceived, we are to use, not a deceitful defense, but a true confession of sins.

14. And some indeed, who are used to excuse their own sins, complain that they are driven to sin by fate, as though the stars had decreed this, and heaven had first sinned by decreeing such, in order that man should after sin by committing such, and thus had rather impute their sin to fortune: who think that all things are driven to and fro by chance accidents, and yet contend that this their wisdom and assertion is not of chance rashness, but of ascertained reason. What madness then is it, to lay to reason their discussions, and to make their actions subject to accidents! Others refer to the devil the whole of what they do ill: and will not have even a share with him, whereas they may suspect whether he by hidden suggestions hath persuaded them to evil, and on the other hand cannot doubt that they have consented to those

suggestions, from whatever source they have come. There are also they who extend their defense of self unto an accusation of God, wretched by the divine judgment, but blasphemers by their own madness. For against Him they bring in from a contrary principle a substance of evil rebelling, which He could not have resisted, had He not blended with that same that was rebelling a portion of His own Substance and Nature, for it to contaminate and corrupt; and they say that they then sin when the nature of evil prevails over the nature of God. This is that most unclean madness of the Manichæans, whose devilish devices the undoubted truth most easily overthrows; which confesses that the nature of God is incapable of contamination and corruption. But what wicked contamination and corruption do they not deserve to have believed of them, by whom God, Who is good in the very highest degree, and in a way that admits not of comparison, is believed to be capable of contamination and corruption?

15. And there are also they who in excuse of their sins so accuse God, as to say that sins are pleasing to Him. For, if they were displeasing, say they, surely by His most Almighty power He would by no means suffer them to take place. As though indeed God suffered sins to be unpunished, even in the case of those whom by remission of sins He frees from eternal punishment! No one forsooth receives pardon of more grievous punishment due, unless he hath suffered some punishment, be it what it may, although far less than what was due: and the fullness of mercy is so conveyed, as that the justice also of discipline is not abandoned. For also sin, which seems unavenged, hath its own attendant punishment, so that

there is no one but by reason of what he hath done either suffers pain from bitterness, or suffers not through blindness. As therefore you say, Why doth He permit those things, if they are displeasing? so I say, Why doth He punish them, if they are pleasing? And thus, as I confess that those things would not take place at all, unless they were permitted by the Almighty, so confess thou that what are punished by the Just One ought not to be done; in order that, by not doing what He punishes, we may deserve to learn of Him, why He permits to exist what He punishes. For, as it is written, "solid food is for the perfect," wherein they who have made good progress already understand, that it pertained rather unto the Almighty power of God, to allow the existence of evils coming from the free choice of the will. So great forsooth is His Almighty goodness, as that even of evil He can make good, either by pardoning, or by healing, or by fitting and turning unto the profit of the pious, or even by most justly taking vengeance. For all these are good, and most worthy a good and Almighty God: and yet they are not made save of evils. What therefore better, what more Almighty, than He, Who, whereas He makes no evil, even of evils makes well? They who have done ill cry unto Him, "Forgive us our debts;" He hears, He pardons. Their own evils have hurt the sinners; He helps and heals their sicknesses. The enemies of His people rage; of their rage He makes martyrs. Lastly, also, He condemns those, whom He judges worthy of condemnation; although they suffer their own evils, yet He doeth what is good. For what is just cannot but be good, and assuredly as sin is unjust, so the punishment of sin is just.

16. But God wanted not power to make man such

as that he should not be able to sin: but He chose rather to make him such, as that it should lie in his power to sin, if he would; not to sin, if he would not; forbidding the one, enjoining the other; that it might be to him first a good desert not to sin, and after a just reward not to be able to sin. For such also at the last will He makes His Saints, as to be without all power to sin. Such forsooth even now hath He His angels, whom in Him we so love, as to have no fear for any of them, lest by sinning he become a devil. And this we presume not of any just man in this mortal life. But we trust that all will be such in that immortal life. For Almighty God Who worketh good even of our evils, what good will He give, when He shall have set us free from all evils? Much may be said more fully and more subtilely on the good use of evil; but this is not what we have undertaken in our present discourse, and we must avoid in it excess of length.

17. Now therefore let us return to that, wherefore we have said what we have. We have need of Continence, and we know it to be a divine gift, that our heart fall not away unto evil words, to make excuses in sins. But what sin is there but that we have need of Continence, to restrain it from being committed, since it is this very Continence which, in case it have been committed, restrains it from being defended by wicked pride? Universally therefore we have need of Continence, in order to turn away from evil. But to do good seems to pertain to another virtue, that is, to righteousness. This the sacred Psalm admonishes us, where we read, "Turn away from evil, and do good." But with what end we do this, it adds bye and bye, saying, "Seek peace, and ensue it." For we shall then have perfect peace, when, our nature

cleaving inseparably to its Creator, we shall have nothing of ourselves opposed to ourselves. This our Savior also Himself would have us to understand, so far as seems to me when He said, "Let your loins be girt, and your lamps burning." What is it, to gird the loins? To restrain lusts, which is the work of continence. But to have lamps burning is to shine and glow with good works, which is the work of righteousness. Nor was He here silent with what end we do these things, adding and saying, "And you like unto men waiting for their Lord, when He cometh from the marriage." But, when He shall have come, He will reward us, who have kept ourselves from those things which lust, and have done those things which charity hath bidden us: that we may reign in His perfect and eternal peace, without any strife of evil, and with the highest delight of good.

18. All we therefore, who believe in the Living and True God, Whose Nature, being in the highest sense good and incapable of change, neither doth any evil, nor suffers any evil, from Whom is every good, even that which admits of decrease, and Who admits not at all of decrease in His own Good, Which is Himself, when we hear the Apostle saying, "Walk in the Spirit, and perform ye not the lusts of the flesh. For the flesh lusted against the Spirit, and the Spirit against the flesh: For these are opposed one to another, that ye do not what ye would." Far be it from us to believe, what the madness of the Manichees believes, that there are here shown two natures or principles contrary one to another at strife, the one nature of good, the other of evil. Altogether these two are both good; both the Spirit is a good, and the flesh a good: and man, who is composed of both, one ruling, the other

obeying, is assuredly a good, but a good capable of change, which yet could not be made save by a Good incapable of change, by Whom was created every good, whether small or great; but how small so ever, yet made by What is Great; and how great so ever, yet no way to be compared with the greatness of the Maker. But in this nature of man, that is good, and well-formed and ordered by One That is Good, there is now war, since there is not yet health. Let the sickness be healed, there is peace. But that sickness fault hath deserved, not nature hath had. And this fault indeed through the laver of regeneration the grace of God hath already remitted unto the faithful; but under the hands of the same Physician nature as yet strives with its sickness. But in such a conflict victory will be entire soundness; and that, soundness not for a time, but forever: wherein not only this sickness is to come to an end, but also none to arise after it. Wherefore the just man addressed his soul and saith, "Bless the Lord, O my soul, and forget not all His returns: Who becomes propitious to all thy iniquities, Who heals all thy sicknesses." He becometh propitious to our iniquities, when He pardons sins: He heals sicknesses when He restrains evil desires. He becometh propitious unto iniquities by the grant of forgiveness: He heals sicknesses, by the grant of continence. The one was done in Baptism to persons confessing; the other is done in the strife to persons contending; wherein through His help we are to overcome our disease. Even now the one is done, when we are heard, saying, "Forgive us our debts;" but the other, when we are heard, saying, "Lead us not into temptation. For everyone is tempted," saith the Apostle James, "being drawn away and enticed by his own lust." And against this fault there is sought the help of medicine from Him, Who can heal all such sicknesses, not by the removal of a nature that is alien from us, but in the renewal of our own nature. Whence also the above-mentioned Apostle saith not, "Everyone is tempted" by lust, but added, "by his own:" that he who hears this may understand, how he ought to cry, "I said, Lord, have mercy upon me, heal my soul, for I have sinned against Thee." For it would not have needed healing, had it not corrupted itself by sinning, so that its own flesh should lust against it, that is, itself should be opposed to itself, on that side, wherein in the flesh it was made sick.

19. For the flesh lusts after nothing save through the soul, but the flesh is said to lust against the spirit, when the soul with fleshly lust wrestles against the spirit. This whole are we: and the flesh itself, which on the departure of the soul dies, the lowest part of us is not put away as what we are to flee from, but is laid aside as what we are to receive again, and, after having received it, never again to leave. But "there is sown an animal body, there shall rise again a spiritual body." Then from that time the flesh will not lust after anything against the spirit, when as itself also shall be called spiritual, forasmuch as not only without any opposition, but also without any need of bodily aliment, it shall be forever made subject unto the spirit, to be quickened by Christ. Therefore these two things, which are now opposed the one to the other within us, since we exist in both, let us pray and endeavor that they may agree. For we ought not to think the one of them an enemy, but the fault, whereby the flesh lusted against the spirit: and this, when healed, will itself cease to exist, and either substance will be safe, and no strife between either. Let us hear the Apostle; "I

know," saith he, "that there dwelleth not in me, that is, in my flesh, any good." This certainly he saith; that the fault of the flesh, in a good thing, is not good; and, when this shall have ceased to exist, it will be flesh, but it will not be now corrupted or faulty flesh. And yet that this pertains to our nature the same teacher shows, by saying, first, "I know that there dwelleth not in me," in order to expound which, he added, "that is, in my flesh, any good." Therefore he saith that his flesh is himself. It is not then itself that is our enemy: and when its faults are resisted, itself is loved, because itself is cared for; "For no one ever hated his own flesh," as the Apostle himself saith. And in another place he saith, "So then I myself with the mind serve the Law of God, but with the flesh the Law of sin." Let them hear that have ears. "So then I myself;" I with the mind, I with the flesh, but "with the mind I serve the Law of God, but with the flesh the law of sin." How "with the flesh the law of sin?" was it at all by consenting unto fleshly lust? Far be it! but by having there motions of desires which he would not have, and yet had. But, by not consenting to them, with the mind he served the Law of God, and kept his members from becoming weapons of sins.

20. There are therefore in us evil desires, by consenting not unto which we live not ill: there are in us lusts of sins, by obeying not which we perfect not evil, but by having them do not as yet perfect good. The Apostle shows both, that neither is good here perfected, where evil is so lusted after, nor evil here perfected, whereas such lust is not obeyed. The one forsooth he shows, where he says, "To will is present with me, but to perfect good is not;" the other, where he says, "Walk in

the Spirit, and perfect not the lusts of the flesh." For neither in the former place doth he say that to do good is not with him, but "to perfect," nor here doth he say, Have not "lusts of the flesh," but "perfect not." Therefore there take place in us evil lusts, when that pleases which is not lawful; but they are not perfected, when evil lusts are restrained by the mind serving the Law of God. And good takes place, when that, which wrongly pleases, takes not place through the good delight prevailing. But the perfection of good is not fulfilled, so long as by the flesh serving the law of sin, evil lust entices, and, although it be restrained, is yet moved. For there would be no need for it to be restrained, were it not moved. There will be at some time also the perfection of good, when the destruction of evil: the one will be highest, the other will be no more. And if we think that this is to be hoped for in this mortal state, we are deceived. For it shall be then, when death shall not be; and it shall be there, where shall be life eternal. For in that world, and in that kingdom, there shall be highest good, no evil: when there shall be, and where there shall be, highest love of wisdom, no labor of continence. Therefore the flesh is not evil, if it be void of evil, that is, of fault, whereby man was rendered faulty, not made ill, but himself making. For on either part, that is, both soul and body, being made good by the good God, himself made the evil, whereby he was made evil. From the guilt of which evil being already also set free through forgiveness, that he may not think what he hath done to be light, he yet wars with his own fault through continence. But far be it that there be any faults in such as reign in that peace which shall be hereafter; since in this state of war there are lessened daily in such as make progress, not sins only, but the very lusts also, with which, by not consenting, we strive, and by consenting unto which we sin.

21. That, therefore, the flesh lusted against the Spirit, that there dwelleth not in our flesh good, that the law in our members is opposed to the law of the mind, is not a mingling of two natures caused of contrary principles, but a division of one against itself caused through desert of sin. We were not so in Adam, before that nature, having listened to and followed its deceiver, had despised and offended its Creator: that is, not the former life of man created, but the latter punishment of man condemned. From which condemnation when set free by Grace, through Jesus Christ, being free they contend with their punishment, having received not as yet full salvation, but already a pledge of salvation: but when not set free, they are both guilty by reason of sins, and involved in punishments. But after this life for the guilty there will remain forever punishment for their crime: for the free there will no more remain forever either crime or punishment: but the good substances, spirit and flesh, will continue forever, which God, Who is good, and incapable of change, created good although capable of change. But they will continue having been changed for the better, never from this time to be changed for the worse: all evil being utterly destroyed, both what man hath unjustly done, and what he hath justly suffered. And, these two kinds of evil perishing utterly, whereof the one is of iniquity going before, the other of unhappiness following after, the will of man will be upright without any depravity. There it will be clear and plain to all, what now many of the faithful believe, few understand, that evil is not a substance: but that, as a wound in a body, so in a

substance, which hath made itself faulty, it hath begun to exist, when the disease hath commenced, and ceased to exist in it, when the healing hath been perfected. Therefore, all evil having arisen from us, and having been destroyed in us, our good also having been increased and perfected unto the height of most happy incorruption and immortality, of what kind shall either of our substances be? forasmuch as now, in this corruption and mortality, when as yet "the corruptible body weighed down the soul;" and, what the Apostle saith, "the body is dead by reason of sin;" yet the same himself bears such witness unto our flesh, that is, to our lowest and earthly part, as to say, what I made mention of a little above, "No one ever hated his own flesh." And to add straightway, "but nourished and cherished it, as also Christ the Church."

22. I say not, therefore, with what error, but with what utter madness, do the Manichees attribute our flesh to some, I know not what, fabled "race of darkness," which they will have hath had its own nature without any beginning ever evil: whereas the true teacher exhorts men to love their own wives by the pattern of their own flesh, and exhorts them unto this very thing by the pattern also of Christ and the Church. Lastly, we must call to mind the whole place itself of the Epistle of the Apostle, relating greatly unto the matter in hand. "Husbands," saith he, "love your wives, as Christ also loved the Church, and delivered Himself up for it, that He might sanctify it, cleansing it by the laver of the water in the word: that He might set forth unto Himself a glorious Church, not having spot, or wrinkle, or any such thing, but that it may be holy and unspotted. So," saith he, "husbands also ought to love their own wives, as their own bodies.

Whoso loveth his own wife, loveth himself." Then he added, what we have already made mention of, "For no man ever hated his own flesh, but nourished it, and cherished it; as also Christ the Church." What saith the madness of most impure impiety in answer to these things? What say ye in answer to these things, ye Manichees; ye who wish to bring in upon us, as if out of the Epistles of the Apostles, two natures without beginning, one of good, the other of evil: and will not listen to the Epistles of the Apostles, that they may correct you from that sacrilegious perverseness? As ye read, "The flesh lusted against the spirit," and, "There dwelleth not in my flesh any good;" so read ye, "No one ever hated his own flesh, but nourished and cherished it, as also Christ the Church." As ye read, "I see another law in my members, opposed to the law of my mind;" so read ye, "As Christ loved the Church, so also ought men to love their own wives, as their own bodies." Be not ye crafty in the former witnesses of Holy Scripture, and deaf in this latter, and ye shall be correct in both. For, if ye receive the latter as right is, ye will endeavor to understand the former also as truth is.

23. The Apostle has made known to us certain three unions, Christ and the Church, husband and wife, spirit and flesh. Of these the former consult for the good of the latter, the latter wait upon the former. All the things are good, when, in them, certain set over by way of pre-eminence, certain made subject in a becoming manner, observe the beauty of order. Husband and wife receive command and pattern how they ought to be one with another. The command is, "Let wives be subject unto their own husbands, as unto the Lord; because the

husband is the head of the wife;" and, "Husbands, love your wives." But there is given a pattern, unto wives from the Church, unto husbands from Christ: "As the Church," saith he, "is subject unto Christ, so also wives unto their own husbands in all things." In like manner also, having given command to husbands to love their own wives, he added a pattern, "As Christ loved the Church." But husbands he exhorted to it from a lower matter also, that is, from their own body: not only from a higher, that is, from their Lord. For he not only saith, "Husbands, love your wives, as Christ also loved the Church," which is from an higher: but he said also, "Husbands ought to love their own wives, as their own bodies," which is from a lower: because both higher and lower are all good. And yet the woman received not pattern from the body, or flesh, to be so subject to the husband as the flesh to the spirit; but either the Apostle would have understood by consequence, what he omitted to state: or haply because the flesh lusted against the spirit in the mortal and sick estate of this life, therefore he would not set the woman a pattern of subjection from it. But the men he would for this reason, because, although the spirit lusted against the flesh, even in this it consults for the good of the flesh: not like as the flesh lusting against the spirit, by such opposition consulted neither for the good of the spirit, nor for its own. Yet the good spirit would not consult for its good, whether by nourishing and cherishing its nature by forethought, or by resisting its faults by continence, were it not that each substance showed God to be the Creator of each, even by the seemliness of this its order. What is it, therefore, that with true madness ye both boast yourselves to be Christians, and with so great, perverseness contend against the Christian Scriptures, with eyes closed, or rather put out, asserting both that Christ hath appeared unto mortals in false flesh, and that the Church in the soul pertains to Christ, in the body to the devil, and that the male and female sex are works of the devil, not of God, and that the flesh is joined unto the spirit, as an evil substance unto a good substance?

24. If what we have made mention of out of the Apostolic Epistles seem to you to fall short of an answer, hear yet others, if ye have ears. What saith the utterly mad Manichæan of the Flesh of Christ? That it was not true, but false. What saith the blessed Apostle to this? "Remember that Christ Jesus rose again from the dead of the seed of David, according to my Gospel." And Christ Jesus Himself saith, "Handle and see, that a spirit hath not flesh and bones, as ye see me to have." How is there truth in their doctrine, which asserts that in the Flesh of Christ there was falsehood? How was there in Christ no evil, in Whom was so great a lie? Because forsooth to men over-clean true flesh is an evil, and false flesh instead of true is not an evil: it is an evil, true flesh of one born of the seed of David, and it is no evil, false tongue of one saying, "Handle, and see, that a spirit hath not flesh and bones, as ye see me to have." Of the Church what saith the deceiver of men with deadly error? That on the side of souls it pertains unto Christ, on the side of bodies unto the devil? What to this saith the Teacher of the Gentiles in faith and truth? "Know ye not," saith he, "that your bodies are members of Christ?" Of the sex of male and female what saith the son of perdition? That either sex is not of God, but of the devil. What to this saith the Vessel of Election? "As," saith he, "the woman from out the man, so also the man through the woman: but all things of God." Of the

flesh what saith the unclean spirit through the Manichæan? That it is an evil substance, and not the creation of God, but of an enemy. What to this saith the Holy Spirit through Paul? "For as the body is one," saith he, "and hath many members, but all the members of the body, being many, are one body: so also is Christ." And a little after; "God hath set," saith he, "the members, each one of them in the body, as He willed." Also a little after; "God," saith he, "hath tempered the body, giving greater honor unto that to which it was wanting, that there should be no schisms in the body, but that the members have the self-same care one for another: and whether one member suffer, all the members suffer with it: or one member be glorified, all the members rejoice with it." How is the flesh evil, when the souls themselves are admonished to imitate the peace of its members? How is it the creation of the enemy, when the souls themselves, which rule the bodies, take pattern from the members of the body, not to have schisms of enmities among themselves, in order that, what God hath granted unto the body by nature, this themselves also may love to have by grace? With good cause, writing to the Romans, "I beseech you," saith he, "brethren, by the mercy of God, that ye present your bodies a sacrifice, living, holy, pleasing to God." Without reason we contend that darkness is not light, nor light darkness, if we present a sacrifice, living, holy, pleasing to God, of the bodies of the "nation of darkness."

25. But, say they, how is the flesh by a certain likeness compared unto the Church? What! doth the Church lust against Christ? whereas the same Apostle said, "The Church is subject unto Christ." Clearly the Church is subject unto Christ; because the spirit therefore

lusted against the flesh, that on every side the Church may be made subject to Christ; but the flesh lusted against the spirit, because not as yet hath the Church received that peace which was promised perfect. And for this reason the Church is made subject unto Christ for the pledge of salvation, and the flesh lusted against the spirit from the weakness of sickness. For neither were those other than members of the Church, unto whom he thus spoke, "Walk in the spirit, and fulfill not the lusts of the flesh. For the flesh lusted against the spirit, and the spirit against the flesh; for these are opposed the one to the other; that ye do not what we would." These things were assuredly spoken unto the Church, which if it were not made subject unto Christ, the spirit would not in it lust against the flesh through continence. By reason of which they were indeed able not to perfect the lusts of the flesh, but through the flesh lusting against the Spirit they were not able to do the things which they would, that is, not even to have the very lusts of the flesh. Lastly, why should we not confess that in spiritual men the Church is subject unto Christ, but in carnal men yet lusted against Christ? Did not they lust against Christ unto whom it was said, "Is Christ divided?" and, "I could not speak unto you as unto spiritual, but as unto carnal. I have given unto you milk to drink as unto babes in Christ, not meat, for ye were not as yet able; but not even now are ye able: for ye are still carnal. For whereas there is among you emulation, and strife, are ye not carnal?" Against whom doth emulation and strife lust, but against Christ? For these lusts of the flesh Christ healed in His own, but loved in none. Whence the holy Church, so long as it hath such members, is not yet without spot or wrinkle. To these are added those other sins also, for which the daily cry of the whole Church is,

"Forgive us our debts:" and, that we should not think spiritual persons exempt from these, not any one so ever of carnal persons, nor anyone so ever of spiritual persons themselves, but he, who lay on the breast of the Lord, and whom He loved before others, saith, "If we shall say that we have not sin, we deceive ourselves, and the truth is not in us." But in every sin, more in what is greater, less in what is less, there is an act of lust against righteousness. And of Christ it is written: "Who was made unto us by God, Wisdom, and Righteous ness, and Sanctification, and Redemption." In every sin therefore without doubt there is an act of lust against Christ. But when He, Who "healed all our sicknesses," shall have led His Church unto the promised healing of sickness, then in none of its members shall there be any, even the very least spot or wrinkle. Then in no way shall the flesh lust against the spirit, and therefore there shall be no cause why the spirit also lust against the flesh. Then all this conflict shall come to an end, then there shall be the highest concord of both substances; then to such a degree shall no one there be carnal, that even the flesh itself shall be spiritual. What therefore each one living after Christ doth with his flesh, whereas he both lusts against its evil lust, which he restrains, hereafter to be healed, which he holds, not yet healed; and yet nourished and cherished its good nature, since "no one ever hated his own flesh," this also Christ doth with the Church, so far as it is lawful to compare lesser with greater matters. For He both represses it with rebukes, that it burst not being puffed up with impunity; and raises it up with consolations, that it sink not being weighed down with infirmity. Hence is that of the Apostle, "For if we would judge ourselves, we should not be judged; but when we are judged, we are rebuked of the

Lord, that we be not condemned with this world." And that in the Psalm, "After the multitude of my griefs in my heart, Thy consolations have gladdened my soul." We are therefore then to hope for perfect soundness of our flesh without any opposition, when there shall be sure security of the Church of Christ without any fear.

26. Thus much will suffice to have treated on behalf of true Continence against the Manichees deceitfully continent, lest the fruitful and glorious labor of Continence, when it restrains and curbs the lowest part of us, that is, the body, from immoderate and unlawful pleasures, be believed not healthfully to chasten, but hostilely to persecute. Forsooth the body is indeed different from the nature of the soul, yet is it not alien from the nature of man: for the soul is not made up of body, but yet man is made up of soul and body: and assuredly, whom God frees, He frees the whole man. Whence our Savior Himself also took upon Him the whole man, having deigned to free in us all that He made. They who hold contrary to this truth, what doth it profit them to restrain lusts? if, that is, they restrain any. What in them can be made clean through Continence, whose such Continence is unclean? and which ought not to be called Continence. Forsooth to hold what they hold is the poison of the devil; but Continence is the gift of God. But as not everyone who suffers anything, or with the greatest endurance suffers any pain whatever, possesses that virtue, which in like manner is the gift of God, and is called Patience; for many endure many torments, in order not to betray either such as are wickedly privy with them in their crimes, or themselves; many in order to satiate glowing lusts, and to obtain, or not to abandon those

things, whereunto they are bound by chain of evil love; many on behalf of different and destructive errors, whereby they are strongly held: of all of whom far be it from us to say that they have true patience: thus not everyone, who contains in anything, or who marvelously retrains even the very lusts of the flesh, or mind, is to be said to possess that continence, of the profit and beauty of which we are treating. For certain, what may seem marvelous to say, through incontinence contain themselves: as if a woman were to contain herself from her husband, because she hath sworn this to an adulterer. Certain through injustice, as if spouse yield not to spouse the due of sexual intercourse, because he or she is already able to overcome such appetite of the body. Also certain contain deceived by false faith, and hoping what is vain, and following after what is vain: among whom are all heretics, and whosoever under the name of religion are deceived by any error: whose continence would be true, if their faith also were true: but, whereas that is not to be called faith, on this account, because it is false; without doubt that also is unworthy the name of continence. For what? are we prepared to call continence, which we must truly say is the gift of God, sin? Far be from our hearts so hateful madness. But the blessed Apostle saith "Everything that is not of faith is sin." What therefore hath not faith, is not to be called continence.

27. There are also they who, in doing open service to evil demons, contain from pleasures of the body, that, through their means, they may satisfy unlawful pleasures, the violence and glow whereof they contain not. Whence also, (to name one case, and pass over the rest in silence by reason of the length of the discourse,) certain come not

near even unto their own wives, whilst, as though clean, they essay through magic arts to gain access unto the wives of others. O marvelous continence, nay rather, singular wickedness and uncleanness! For, if it were true continence, the lust of the flesh ought rather to contain from adultery, than, in order to commit adultery, from marriage. Forsooth marriage continence is wanting to ease this lust of the flesh, and to check its curb but thus far, that neither in marriage itself it run riot by immoderate license, but that a measure be observed, either such as is due to the weakness of the spouse, unto whom the Apostle enjoins not this, as of command, but yields it as of permission; or such as is suited for the begetting of sons, which was formerly the one alone occasion of sexual intercourse to both holy fathers and mothers. But continence doing this, that is, moderating, and in a certain way limiting in married persons the lust of the flesh, and ordering in a certain way within fixed limits its unquiet and inordinate motion, uses well the evil of man, whom it makes and wills to make perfect good: as God uses even evil men, for their sake whom He perfects in goodness.

28. Far be it therefore that we say of continence, of which Scripture saith. "And this very thing was wisdom, to know whose gift it was," that even they possess it, who, by containing, either serve errors, or overcome any lesser desires for this purpose, that they may fulfill others, by the greatness of which they are overcome. But that continence which is true, coming from above, wills not to repress some evils by other evils, but to heal all evils by goods. And, briefly to comprehend its mode of action, it is the place of continence to keep watch to restrain and heal all delights whatsoever of lust, which

are opposed to the delight of wisdom. Whence without doubt they set it within too narrow bounds, who limit it to restraining the lusts of the body alone: certainly they speak better, who say that it pertains to Continence to rule in general lust or desire. Which desire is set down as a fault, nor is it only of the body, but also of the soul. For, if the desire of the body be in fornications and drunkennesses; hard enmities, strifes, emulations, lastly, hatreds, their exercise in the pleasure of the body, and not rather in the motion and troubled states of the soul? Yet the Apostle called all these "works of the flesh," whether what pertained to the soul, or what pertained properly to the flesh, calling forsooth the man himself by the name of the flesh. Forsooth they are the works of man, whatsoever are not called works of God; forasmuch as man, who does these, lives after himself, not after God, so far as he does these. But there are other works of man, which are rather to be called works of God. "For it is God," saith the Apostle, "Who worketh in you both to will and to do, according to His good pleasure." Whence also is that, "For as many as are led by the spirit of God, these are sons of God."

29. Thus the spirit of man, cleaving unto the Spirit of God, lusts against the flesh, that is, against itself: but for itself, in order that those motions, whether in the flesh or in the soul, after man, not after God, which as yet exist through the sickness man hath gotten, may be restrained by continence, that so health may be gotten; and man, not living after man, may now be able to say, "But I live, now not I, but there lives in me Christ." For where not I, there more happily I: and, when any evil motion after man arises, unto which he, who with the mind serves the Law

of God, consents not, let him say that also, "Now it is not I that do this." To such forsooth are said those words, which we, as partners and sharers with them, ought to listen to. "If ye have risen together with Christ, seek the things that are above, where Christ is sitting at the Right Hand of God: mind the things that are above, not what are upon earth. For ye are dead, and your life is hid with Christ in God: when Christ your life shall have appeared, then ye also shall appear with Him in glory." Let us understand unto whom he is speaking, yea, rather, let us listen with more attention. For what more plain than this? what more clear? He is certainly speaking unto those, who had risen again with Christ, not yet surely in the flesh, but in the mind: whom he calls dead, and on this account the more living: for "your life," saith he, "is hid with Christ in God." Of such dead the speech is: "But I live, now not I, but there lives in me Christ." They therefore, whose life was hidden in God, are admonished and exhorted to mortify their members, which are upon the earth. For this follows, "Mortify, therefore, your members, which are upon the earth." And, lest any through excess of dullness should think that such are to mortify the members of the body that are seen, straightway opening what it is he saith, "Fornication," saith he, "uncleanness, passion, evil lust, and covetousness, which is idolatry." But is it so to be believed, that they, who were already dead, and their life hidden with Christ in God, were still committing fornication, were still living in unclean habits and works, were still slaves to passions of evil lust and covetousness? What madman would thus think of such? What, therefore, would he that they mortify, save the motions themselves still living in a certain intrusion of their own, without the consent of our mind, without the action of the members of the body? And how are they mortified by the work of continence, save when we consent not to them with the mind, nor are the members of the body yielded to them as weapons; and, what is greater, and to be looked to with yet greater watchfulness of continence, our very thought itself, although in a certain way it be touched by their suggestion, and as it were, whisper, yet turns away from these, that it receive not delight from them, and turns to more delightful thoughts of things above: on this account naming them in discourse, that men abide not in them, but flee from them. And this is brought to pass, if we listen effectually, with His help, Who, through His Apostle gives this command, "Seek things that are above, where Christ is sitting at the Right Hand of God. Mind the things that are above, not what are on earth."

30. But, after that he had made mention of these evils, he added and said, "On account of which cometh the wrath of God on the sons of unbelief." Surely it was a wholesome alarm that believers might not think that they could be saved on account of their faith alone, even although they should live in these evils: the Apostle James with most clear speech crying out against that notion, and saying, "If any say that he have faith, and have not works, shall his faith be able to save him?" Whence also here the Teacher of the Gentiles said, that on account of these evils the wrath of God cometh on the sons of unbelief. But when he saith, "Wherein ye also walked sometime, when ye were living therein;" he shows sufficiently that now they were not living therein. Forsooth unto these they had died, that their life might be hidden in God with Christ. When then they were now not living in them, they were now bidden to mortify such.

Forsooth, themselves not living in the same, the things were living, as I have already shown a little above, and were called their members, that is to say, those faults which dwelt in their members; by a way of speech, that which is contained through that which contains; as it is said, The whole Forum talks of it, when men talk who are in the Forum. In this very way of speech it is sung in the Psalm, "Let all the earth worship Thee:" that is, all men who are in the earth.

31. "But now do ye also," saith he, "put down all;" and he makes mention of several more evils of that sort. But what is it, that it is not enough for him to say, "Do ye put down all," but that he added the conjunction and said, "ye also?" save that lest they should not think that they did those evils and lived in them with impunity on this account, because their faith set them free from wrath, which cometh upon the sons of unbelief, doing these things, and living in them without faith. Do ye also, saith he, put down those evils, on account of which cometh the wrath of God on the children of unbelief; nor promise yourselves impunity of them on account of merit of faith. But he would not say, "put ye down," unto those who had already laid down so far as that they consented not to such faults, nor were yielding their members to them as weapons of sin, save that the life of Saints stands in this past deed, and is still engaged in this work, so long as we are mortal. For, so long as the Spirit lusted against the flesh, this business proceeds with great earnestness, resistance is offered unto evil delights, unclean lusts, carnal and shameful motions, by the sweetness of holiness, by the love of chastity, by spiritual vigor, and by the beauty of continence; thus they are laid down by them

who are dead to them, and who live not in them by consenting. Thus, I say, they are put down, whilst they are weighed down by continued continence, that they rise not again. Whosoever, as though secure, shall cease from this laying aside of them, straightway they will assault the Citadel of the mind, and will themselves put it down thence, and will reduce it into slavery to them, captive after a base and unseemly fashion. Then sin will reign in the mortal body of man to obey its desires; then will it yield its members weapons of unrighteousness unto sin: and the last state of that man shall be worse than the former. For it is much more tolerable not to have begun a contest of this kind, than after one hath begun to have left the conflict, and to have become in place of a good warrior, or even in place of a conqueror, a captive. Whence the Lord saith not, whoso shall begin, but "Whoso shall persevere unto the end, he shall be saved."

32. But whether keenly contending, that we be not overcome, or overcoming diverse times, or even with unhoped and unlooked for ease, let us give the glory unto Him Who giveth continence unto us. Let us remember that a certain just man said, "I shall never be moved:" and that it was showed him how rashly he had said this, attributing as though to his own strength, what was given to him from above. But this we have learnt from his own confession: for soon after he added, "Lord, in Thy will Thou hast given strength to my beauty; but Thou hast turned away Thy Face, and I was troubled." Through a remedial Providence he was for a short time deserted by his Ruler, in order that he might not himself through deadly pride desert his Ruler. Therefore, whether here, where we engage with our faults in order to subdue and

make them less, or there, as it shall be in the end, where we shall be void of every enemy, because of all infection, it is for our health that we are thus dealt with, in order that, "whoso glories, he may glory in the Lord."

www.ingramcontent.com/pod-product-compliance
Lightning Source LLC
Chambersburg PA
CBHW052044070526
44584CB00018B/2602